The Book of Tides

GW00497934

The Book of Tides

Angela Readman

Nine
Arches
Press

The Book of Tides
Angela Readman

ISBN: 9781911027102

Cover artwork: 'Boat' (lithograph, 2011) © C.A. Hiley
www.cahiley.com

First published November 2016 by:

Nine Arches Press
PO Box 6269
Rugby
CV21 9NL
United Kingdom

www.ninearchespress.com

Printed in Britain by:
The Russell Press Ltd.

Nine Arches Press is supported using public funding by the National Lottery through Arts Council England.

Contents

'If you don't become the ocean, you'll be seasick everyday'

– Leonard Cohen

The Book of Tides

Like that, the old lass could switch into a ship's mast,
stood on that cliff, air wringing a swell of hips
out of her skirt. Then, she was Ma again,
dragging me through the plothery snicket,
back to the cottage. Outside tinkled and strode.
Fishermen knocked, bags of whelks at the door,
trout like rainbows dandled in raw hands.
                                    Aye,
the woman had a knack for the wind, knew it,
whisper to gale. She got weather the way a mute
woman, married forever, spoke to her husband
without saying a word. I did not know if I'd live
my magic too, if I'd ever cut through the bluster
and blow in an ear to know when to will
a man home or wreck him en route.
                                    Flick,
flick, at licked pages in her big Book of Tides,
I watched her spit and tie the sky up, a snap
of fringe knotted into a handkerchief slipped
into a breast pocket. Sometimes she stared
at wolves chasing the window, landlocked clouds
circled the house. The ships sailed right enough.
Fingers in pockets stroked our blood knots
like starved birds pecking for scraps of a heart.

In the Absence of Mary

I have taken to wearing a blue shift
to absorb the look in your eyes, ever since

that afternoon you spoke of being chosen.
The daylily stars on the ledge softening

their points, only hours left. Once more,
we uncovered our hair, streams

no one had yet followed to the arch
of our backs, clinging to our damp necks.

No more would we dream of the sea,
stepping into that deadness to feel

our limbs lift. Salt lipped, afloat
on a surge of what women should be.

I carried the linen with you to the line,
aware of a rustle of doves in the olives,

shuffles of feather whispering *what if...*
Holding sheets to the sun, you grew wings.

I stepped into your shadow, overlapped,
already knowing later I would sit

where you sat, count a cross-stitch of stars,
and stuff the shawl you left up my dress.

Featherweight

The farrier hands me a stone like an egg, clefted, heart-shaped enough. I pocket it, laden with love. On the way home, I rush past a hush of reeds and picture a walk down the aisle. We'll marry on a Monday when the church costs less. I will wear a plain shift, loaded with only one shade of white, watermarks ironed off my back.

Outside the woodshed, Mother bites the webs of her hands to black scabs. I nod. We speak only hisses. Our eyes are varnish, keep what we don't say intact. She knew it was coming. I'm old enough. Eventually I was going to be loved. She lights the swan skin. It burns like a sigh. The air plucks smoky strands, wisps dust a chalked moon.

The skin felt too big, hand-me-down feathers too heavy for flight. Then, it fit like a blizzard, down between my legs tickled my petticoat to shreds, swept my skinny legs up. It was the same for her, I suppose – all this flying and loving and not knowing how to stop. The steel of our wings can break first love's back – we do not know our span. Boys who got too close snapped, spines skinny rushes whistling in the wind.

The skin spits. Mother pokes ash, her neck is a coat hook hanging up the moonlight.

I, too, will marry a man who never saw me as a swan. He will not know as birds we miss nothing. Yet when he kisses me, softly, woman, I miss my beak.

The Museum of Water

There is nothing we keep to remember
but water, our wavering wall of bottles

and vials. Ripples of sun let the room shiver
whenever a door slams. We dip into drops

of light and feel we could drown. One
by one, we lift glassware and peer in at life

distilled: fingers of font, an hour we bathed
in love – soapy as a pearl crushed,

returning to the source that made it shine.
Our tears don't look like much, barely fill

a hotel pot of jam. We lay them down
beside rain, bottles we clutched for our life

at the foot of a memory we hadn't yet climbed,
as if knowing we would soon need the mist

on someone's hair, beads of cold showers,
the blood of a snowman that melted so fast,

to splash on our faces, and drink,
drink until we are something like full.

The Morning of La Llorona

After the drowning, I lay my palms on the table
and watched my fingers soak into dead wood,
I saw the grain lighten, my old hands draining away.

I untied my apron like a raft the colour of fire.
It couldn't save us. Cotton roses drifted, moved
to bits by my hips, the white water of my neck.

I was a woman of water, foremost. I fed my girls
little birds, silver flecks off the mirror. I killed
a kingfisher, sliced light off its back to fill gaps.

Yet under my dress was a river – a bellyful of notes
in bottles, so many men I almost loved unread.
I thought of you, your good hand undoing my braid.

To see you, I made a dress. I tore scraps off the sky
each night you weren't there, pinned it to my chest.
I wore it with pearls on my wrists, bubbles of air.

And I rushed to your house, a waterfall, ready
to pour whoever I thought I was into your arms.

The Woman Who Could Not Say Love

If there's a more fluent way to write it
than with steel, a needle held
to the window, looping an apostrophe

of sunlight to his coat,
she doesn't know it. Let a stitch
in a frayed pocket proclaim

what thinking of him is. Night
trawling, allow him to plunge his hands
out of the cold, feel the ruck –

one silk knot in the cloth
puckering up to his finger
in the coarse dark.

The Herring Lass and the Soap

The herring roll off the boat, an oil-crested
wave on the dock. I scrape knives on whetstone,
slash flour sacks, bind the clooties to my hands.

I carry my soap on a string, its blade jabs
my sternum, baits me into wondering if my fingers
looked wounded stroking a man on a Sunday.

The school of him slipped over me, in,
delivering a lesson about skin. The hut stank
of a midnight catch, rug riddled in silverfish,

clothes a pool by my kist. I can't get naked
without gutting myself – a shoal of workdays swim.
He washed me from my toes to my kerbies,

then started again. Each night is a sliver since.
I hold soap to a candle, my stained glass window
to the one moment I was clean. It feels like the bone

of a minute someone managed to get inside me:
I was a smokehouse being filled with sweet peas.

Radiography

He lifts the picture of her bones
to the light, holds it close to the bulb

to show me my mother full of leaves
in autumn, baring the steel

of their scaffolding to the wind.
And I want to hold him

for tickling streams with a stick,
cracks in the lake I've skated for years,

felt split under my feet. I didn't know
inside her would look so beautiful,

cool as spilled ink, a cyanotype of years,
those shadows in her head the shape

of a polar bear sniffing an evening,
nosing through the ice.

The Fisher Daughter

Don't rub the collar of a sailor, that cloth of dusks won't wash.
Never say break a leg, unless you're willing to do the job.
Don't look at crows on the dock, avoid curates. Look a magpie
in the eye, salute the cassock stapled to its back. Don't wink
at a man; never drink from the bottle, unless you can finish the lot.
Don't sail on a Monday, Cain slew Abel. Stop growing so fast
your sister's clothes won't fit. Never step on a ship if you're a girl,
give birth on a ship for luck. Don't sit like that, cross your legs.
Don't sneeze up a fog, whistle at the world's expense. Don't
let the dog sniff the tackle. Never worry a ladder in a stocking.
Fix the nets. Don't forget your handkerchief. Tie a knot in it, drop
it from the landing and release swallows to fly alongside the fleet.
Never get married, listen to your Ma. Don't love a man too much
– stuff a swan feather in his pillow if you want him to fly home.
You can't spell women without omen. Don't speak to your father
before a catch. Watch your mother blurt the weather is fine
and look for something to undo the bad luck. The woman picks
up a pin and holds out a finger. The man sticks it in, draws blood.
Don't blink, see how everything is done and almost undone,
known and unknown. Feel free to think you won't need this later on.

The House that Wanted to be a Boat

The cottage slips a little each day,
closer to the cliff. We picture it as a boat,

drifting off in one piece as we carry
out spoons, china cups, and stand back.

It should leap into the void, skinny dip
like a woman realising she can dive.

Yet it slides slowly, glacial
pools of one man's fingertips glossed

into skirting boards hold it back. Strands
of his hair fasten floorboards that keel

for our losses. Mother's face is a gable,
wallpaper still hanging on, plaster ducks

on the wall pointing out all this space
on our backs. There is nothing to do

but stare as the roof tips its hat.
Bricks buckle up, and freefall.

The Aerialist's Shopping List

the shiver of a balloon puckering up
        before it drifted – string snapped,
I want it back. I need intakes of breath
      I loaned flaming birthday cakes.
Feathers, pleating my view of the eaves,
       my atlas is swallows
breaking out of the cracks.
                   Dragonflies dip
into my juice glass and I'd kill for them.
      I crawl into striped tights
like a bolt of wasps. Give me air, blows
I donated to a dying man on the street,
              palms
levelling my load. I did not crack
a rib. Let me be a disposable tissue, rolling
         in the wind,
carrying my mother's tears to the gulley.
washing each one clean. The prayer to Saint Rita
    she kept in her purse, frittered
by the church wall like snowflakes
        building a quietude.
Let me, just once, be a bird, deft –
    picking up paper pieces, adding full stops
to my nest. I eat wings, just to keep reaching
for a hand that has dropped me before.

The Long April of Electra

With more than one way to kill a mother,
I plot to love her. Our smiles are pearl shivs,
father wounds we may not find for years.

I've learnt to whistle like a God breathing
prophecies into chimney pots, cut to the nerve.
I step into tender seconds, trying on her shoes.

Lifting a moth off her robe, I recall a time
she braided Cassandra's hair. Knuckles half-moons,
floating on, swallowed by a river of oil.

The afternoon is spilt lemonade in her room
full of *him*, squeezing a woman from a clay figure
set to be widow – zest at her lips, wine pressed

from wry grapes. The sheets are a field, ploughed
by a man who never fought a war – sweat
decorating his chest in gold chains for her hands.

I fill the urn. The daffodils I place by her bed
all April are yellow horses, sniffing Trojans,
waiting to charge through the walls.

Breaking into the Convent

I keep coming back to the convent anyway.
I finger a ladder of rain in dry stone
as if touching the stocking of a saint.

A rustle of nuns in the orchard
grace apples with the shadows of hands,
slender as spiders navigating the globe

and from the window, a steady *chop chop*
sugared by laughter. Women breast-polish
bruises and pare skin with small knives

to find their gods. I'd kill for that – to sing,
work, fall to my knees and find the holiness
of everything. I have a strong breadknife,

a crow bar, photographs of everyone
I ever kissed, and did not. These, I shower,
over the wall, a blizzard of mouths I let lie

with crackling blossom hugging the lawn.
Once more, I take off my clothes and try
the gate, carrying my suitcase laden with air.

To Kill a Robin

Come January, the pair of us clarted out to pluck
the morning, feet bound in brushwood – plumage
flying out of my Mother's mouth. It was us
or the birds. If you kill a robin on New Year's Day,
give a feather to a rodman and he'll always sail clear.
She would not be a widow, not yet. You could say
I had a mind for the birds, the hunch of me
hunkered in spitting distance of the river, so still
and part of everything in my brown coat, I wanted
to grab my cold breath and pull it back in.
Ma stood listening for the *tek tek*, a cough hanging
frayed streamers over our heads. I caught the robin
in nithered fingers I barely dared open. There,
the bird perfectly refused to have its neck snapped.
It simply stopped in the cave of my grasp, one
last trill like water rolling a silence over my hands.

My Father Snaps off Mermaids like Porn

And we're here again, kicking at Sunday's door,
bloated with autumn, we jab into the shed
stashing our secrets like diamonds in apple crates.
Dad swipes an arc of sun to the window, cobwebs
lacing his cuff. He grasps the rasp and I sit.

The nailbrush on the ledge concedes like a kid
with a Mohawk parted for church. Scrit, scrit…
I listen to the colours on the paint cans spill over
and gloss themselves shut. The scales fly, sequin
rakes, spades, fling pearls at a saw's rusty tooth.

I stare at blood on my legs, a join-the-dots of my life.
Because it's not for us, Son, this merman stuff, sackless
drifters, our junk in a glittery purse. I open the door.
My father follows, cuts a finger on the knob and holds
up a scale like filed rain. We will find them all year.

Two Hundred Snow Geese

The day the geese fell into the lake, one,
another, a steel fork of flight rattling out
of air, interlocked as a drawer of cutlery,

she folded herself into the log pile.
Umbrella defeated, the skein falling
onto crabgrass, carrying the sound

of a thousand winter trees shaking off
a burden of snow. So soft, they looked
still, breast plump full of twilights, pockets

of breezes on other islands. And so loud,
even in death, steely wings torpedoes,
the quiet around his house shrapnel.

Couldn't say why she decided right then,
she wouldn't see in another spring with him,
or why she stayed crouched for so long.

Plotting her path through snow banks
of bird, she pictured the mainland,
the size of the steps she'd have to take.

What the Sindy House Taught Me

There will be doors you cannot open,
views printed to the windows endlessly.

You can be surrounded by antiques,
but be unable to peel the bone china off

the dresser. Almost nothing can be held
in your hands. You can sit anywhere,

with legs that don't always bend, sleep
with open eyes. Some curtains won't close.

Your clothes won't fit in the wardrobe,
some dresses you'll never get into

unless someone screws off your head –
if they're bored enough they'll put it back on.

You will get a bad haircut, someone who looks
like you used to will sit on your patio as you lie

outside naked. She is waiting for a man
to knock on her cardboard door. Carefully,

watch him not fit in the lift, float up, and in.
This is why her house has only three walls.

When We Don't Talk About the Weather

The moon washes up to the window as you undress.
Outside, fishermen haul out the stars in their nets.
The sheets are an albatross, flapping over us. You dive
into bed, a billow rocking the vessel I live in.
Tonight I lose men to love you like this.
Other people's sons drown between my legs.
I forget to blow a kiss at the clouds for the ones
who pressed whispers onto my salty lips.
You lap me up like a drunk, open-mouthed for rain.
And I keen, the knot of me untied, absent loves
unmoored into storms without the anchor of a thought.
The breakers foam with boy spit, carry bones
ashore. Bladderwrack wraps lost lips in a bow,
sea snails scrawl apologies all over blue tongues.

The Tattooist's Daughter

Every time she wants to recall her mother's eyes, she rolls up his sleeve and stares at the swallow flying over the milk of his wrist. The feathers are the colour of dish-cloths, a freckle of ink floats on a vein.

You have to lose an arm and a leg to be an artist, her father says. Come face-to-face with your mistakes whenever you bathe.

There isn't an inch of himself he can reach that isn't coated in kittiwakes, roses, dancing girls that bleed, scab and heal. And still, he strips off a sock, contorts to practise on the ball of his foot, deciding one second at a time if it tickles or hurts.

It was simpler with a wife, a body stocking of ink. He silked all the places she wanted to go all over her. He'd find her staring in the mirror like a map, stroking a palm tree on her thigh.

He can't hold his tongue as steady as a needle. The girl ironed his shirt, scorched a cuff. Now silence lingers like char. There is only one way to say *I forgive you* for some.

Just like her mother, she stretches a bare arm through the space where words hang. Fourteen, her skin is a pale apology she rolls out when she must. One arm on the table, she waits to see acceptance take the form of a turtle this time.

The Preacher's Son and the Beard of Bees

The July my father died I separated the hive,
fed his bees sugar syrup, platitudes and Amens.

The queen hung in a glass vial around my neck
in the orangery. I couldn't smell myself in his shirt.
Collar a leash starched to my neck, his cologne peered

over my shoulder and battled the jasmine outside.
I felt the congregants nibble bat shapes into bread
in the house. The wet weight of Mother's black dress

choking a chorus of sobs out of her, his final sermon.
I closed my eyes, so awake I had to fake something
like death to hear my heart chipping at my chest.

The swarm began to flow uphill, a dark lace
over the apple stuck in my throat. Insects climbed
my chin and read the pale hieroglyph of a scar,

its buckle shape, out loud. I felt legs prick to life
every nerve on my face as I stood imperfectly still.

At Six Stone, I Think of Feeding the Birds

Whenever I lay on the bed for you, stark,
I picture setting a table, stroking crinkles

out of the cloth. I am a hostess presenting
china bowls I carry in the hollows of my hips,

I want only to see you bow your head. I sip
the second a man can make me think of birds,

so delicate, pecking my skin as if I was
a porcelain dish a kiss could crack. It's of no matter

if I haven't eaten all week. I have your hair,
the scent of it wafts into me like bread, fills me up.

You can picture a church, if you gaze up at my ribs,
an archway where you can hear your voice echo

right through me, if you listen. It moves
like a pigeon locked in a vestibule.

Kissing the Man with the Beard of Bees

There's small life in the sugar bowl.
The waitress parts grains with a spoon, lifts

insect and bowl to the door and pours
a pale storm into the cracked cup of the day.

She has called no one anything but honey all year,
fur grazes an ear, wings comb her hair, she brushes

a bee on its way. Once, she almost kissed a man
with a beard of bees, when she was a girl

and he was a boy, a flock of sunlight whiskering
his chin, lips underlined by a scar waxing a story

he never shared to his face. Tonight she drives
by him, a man with a crawling beard on Route 56.

She stares at the fuzzy spot she could almost taste
a veil of possibility. He stands stone still, smells

honey, just where her lips once placed his name,
a zillion felt fingertips caress it, dangle their sting.

Woman and Rat

It's just us and nettles serrating
the wind. Me and the rat in the drum,
lid covered, floating nose down.

For days I've ignored it, a skitter
of death dropped into my lap. Fur
the colour of cloud shift, autumn

spraying its name over our heads.
I stare at the rat swollen as a balloon.
Tail flexing scales to the tune of old rain

dripping off the shed into a pool.
It looks nothing like a creature
I should run from now, no more

than a ball, except for its paws,
foxglove pink, stuck to its bloat
like an afterthought of suede gloves

left on a bench. The child's fishing net
I hold is too small, my hands so bare
I can't grasp a tail. So I stare, nettles

kissing my legs awake, as I flip
the drum lid and fling my shivers
into the river over the fence.

Our Names in Pebbles

Our lives are salvage, on the glint of a storm
we fly out of the house like booted angels,
a clink of gates our splintered wings.

The barrels are always gone, old men roll
home, fires in whiskers, breath bobbing
for kisses their wives have yet to learn.

We hold driftwood like a flame to the notion
of winter, so slippery in our grip. Back, forth,
back, we cart in the dusk, our shifting not done,

we sign our names in stones on planks. Ours
is written in mussels, brittle as lasses in aprons
queuing for milk, satin petticoats under silt skirts.

Mother makes a row of shells and cops a glance
of my father lugging a ship's desk for a widow
– seaweed legged, drawer full of crabs.

Tonight I'll see her circle, ladling soup, so close
he may feel a kiss sail over his neck, she'll lean in
clank a pocket and lay a single shell on his wrist.

Circe Sings to the Pigs

It ain't hard to make a pig serenade you,
all you need is a bucket full of yesterday,
slops to strike with a spoon. And song

is a dirt storm, the pigs run to me
blissful, uncertain as girls in new shoes.
Brighter than wet battlefields,

the pomegranates they smash, seeds
slicked to their snouts. I sing to the pigs
whatever I like. Some are so small,

they sup at a goat bladder of milk. Others,
sing of the sunrise a hog must carry in his ears
into night. These are the animals that hear

the day fade, yet can only dig up a sonata
of grunt, hoik and groin for whoever
brings the grub. I hum to their tails

about fingers losing themselves in long curls,
snouts in my palm snuffly juveniles snorting
steam rings onto a courtesan's window.

I sing of love, the creatures offer no answer.
This is when I enjoy their company the most.

The Honey Jar

It squats in a cupboard like a stopwatch –
his last jar of honey, immune to winter.
The cold days we ached for spoonfuls of summer

to glide down our throats. I carry it, glassy
fingers clouding the hour my father stood still,
under the moving fur coat of the grist.

He moved those frames like still lives of himself.
I recall him as I lift the lid, a compass of drips
stuck on one day I saw the man on his knees.

The hive scumbled in static, dead for no reason
we understood, he brought an orange bucket
and scooped up fistfuls of bees, a sound soft

as chrysanthemums falling off the stem, laid
in the not quite autumn sun. I open my mouth
and let a viscous rain of things I'd forgotten fall.

Knuckles buried in hush, suddenly so small
for a man of his size, pale as china hands
holding on to scraps of August's dusk.

The Orange I Didn't Give the Girl Driving the Tram

comes with me to war, still in my pocket,
a small sun I didn't push through the window

of the tram. I did not smile at the driver;
it is not what we do. We wait to see if

a girl will slow down, stop long enough
for a tokko tai to run, catch up and get on.

I hold the fruit on the plane, a planet
under my thumb, fizzing like the laughter

of a serious girl. Try not to think of her peeling
it cautiously, juice racing down her sleeve.

The pith clings to my cuff, firm as a cobweb
over a back door, a picture of a woman

with fruit-wrinkled fingers, combing her hair
behind an ear, brushing the sleet off my coat.

Lady with a Goose on her Head

No one carries a still wing as well as the lady
with a goose on her head. In the market, ducks

dangle by the crop. She walks on, her posture
is a girl balancing books. I heard woman and bird

became friends after it quit laying eggs, waddled
up to her door, a pick of crumbs on the mat. I hear

she's a widow, *and* I hear she never married. Love
was a kamikaze at war. I can't ask. She has ears

only for the common grey goose, gabbling its view
of stone clouds and hail. Each morning she passes

in a red coat, buys a quince and strolls on, a smile
she won't give just anyone folded into feet vividly

paddling nowhere, infinite stories webbed to her lips.
It's possible she's poor, or invented the biro I use.

Only one thing is clear: she has a goose. It won't leave.
It flies so completely in the air she wraps around herself.

Hallelujah for 50ft Women

Hallelujah to lasses who got too big for their boots,
and stepped outside the fitting rooms of their Mother's eyes.

Their breasts pocket tattoos of anyone who skipped
a beat. You'll spot such a girl, strolling on: 50ft tall,
a milkman's moon spotting sequins on her skirt.

You don't have to know if she's going dancing too soon,
or skated over the hours you slept. She will look
through flat windows at her sunburnt neighbours,
faces pink as the contents of a bubblegum machine.

You may feel the girl's sigh make your furniture
paper. It is a dollhouse, our world. She breathes
and everything moves. Try to keep up to her stride.

Consider the size of the act of her crushing no one,
carefully side-stepping policemen, helmets glinting
bottle caps, megaphones like flies. There's no weapon

she can drop. She has none but herself, fingers
trailing frosty hotel roofs like wedding cakes left out
for pigeons. Put faith in the smallness of yourself,

sweat by the quay as she slips off her shoes, cools
a foot in the river outside the opera house – a mirror
for fog and sky-fancying girls. Be like the gulls, coast
on the waves her toes dip and dab, cry her praises.

Be afraid, one move can kill us. Call her name.
Let us be ants on her palm, lifted to meet her eye.

If I Let You Film Me...

even when I am still, I'll be moving somewhere.
I'll be alive in the kitchen, washing dishes,

as if they're my face. Yet, somewhere I will be
doing things that look like a woman in love.

I'll do you like an item on a list I'll never complete.
Your shirt will be endless, folded around me,

a tent of notions of girls who lay here before,
careful as picnics on lawns. You'll say I am beautiful

and I'll believe it, just once, a million times,
already pressing pause on your mouth as you speak,

rewinding to a second when our picture is perfect.
I do not look like a bad feminist in the lens, lifting

my shirt as if receiving sunburn. You simply look
like a man who must catch that look on my face

before it's aware it exists, fights itself like koi in a mirror.
There will always be somewhere you can arrange me

simply as flowers. Be the vase. If I let you film me,
one day we'll see love when we've forgotten how it's done.

The Religion of Mermaids

There's nothing to pray to, but the rain skinny-dipping
on my legs, fusing into one drop where they meet.
I thought that's how love was. That it meant severing
a smoking tail to find the hole in me, learning
to walk as if any stagger may turn into a waltz. I try.
There's always the dew to baptise myself in, ripples
of my reflection aged in the well. And still, that man
to praise gutting cod, a sling of spines like spent wishes.
I stroke the cat. Winter offers us communion, fins
iced to the steel bucket I carry inside. If I search,
I can find the tide in all things, really, let the steam
on the windows weep on my behalf. Even skins
are a blessing I peel off the counter. They stick to me
like an off-cut of siren leather, pieced into a glove.

Backendish

The feeling slides over you, the sun slots
low between the terraces and scores
a worth to the windows, flaking gold.

Mother kicks her sandals under the stairs
and scrolls on canary socks like a skin
that refuses to let the dark nights seep in.

This is your last chance to sit outside
as you are, bare arms spotting a chill,
skin puckering up to short days ahead.

Your face is a flicker already, drawn
by the gas fire, the rag bag spilling
your mother's previous lives on the rug.

Even now, with so few red leaves on the ash
you know you'll lose count. Girls roll a tab,
smoke an air-show of their boyfriends' names.

You sit on the step, your mother's scissors
inside, chasing lace on a wedding dress
to stitch onto winter's tablecloth.

The Sound of a Knot Being Untied

Look to your lasses, lads, if you can.
Fingers slick with the art of her spit,
she shushes out lamps and flaps
on a nightgown before the candle is lit.
You may wonder when being naked stopped
being as simple as catching a woman bathe
– raindrops hung on the line as water rolled,
anchored a collarbone to a pulse. You'll
remember the snow the winter you wed,
moths at the shutters, a shy wife pulling
an eiderdown over a breast. The pale of her
skin seemed to spill out and lay on the cottage roofs,
shush horse prints and boots in the clarts.
The same woman can turn her back now
and sigh scythes of frost to the window.
Look, listen to slow combs of hair, strands
flying at bristles – a lightning in the room.
She scrapes soap off her wedding ring,
unknots a scarf and slips it over the silver, sly
as cloud across the moon. Look to that lass, now,
open a mouthful of sorrys, kiss her while you can.

*Fishermen once held the superstition that some women could
prevent storms by tying knots in a handkerchief, such handkerchiefs
were carried for a safe voyage.*

The Woman Who Could Not Say Goodbye

He'll come to hear it soon enough, by the door
where a woman can simply put herself out with the milk.

The air there is ivory, cool as a piano key worn
by notions of leaving that didn't play out. It is not a sole

act, farewell, but a language slow as wood smoke
doving the wall over the hearth. He'll come to learn

the so longs she laid all around the house. Carved
into couches, an embrace of absence, sags where he can sit

and observe her slow bow, stowed in the snowdrops
she placed in a vase. So suddenly, the clothes lines

look like unwritten confessions in diaries. The horizon is
a closed ballroom where days of the week refuse to dance.

The Tendering

It was simple with him at six on the dot,
to put on the kettle, fetch a bowl and gather

his hands for the tendering. Jug lifted,
she saw his fingers breathe underwater, hot

as he could stand. Next, a needle kissing
the flame of a gas ring, a spelk of lamplight

in her grip – chasing the graft dashed
into his lifeline. He suckled seeds she left

in his fist like a lamb at the strawberries.
Those splinters on her cloth looked like nothing,

so slight it took forty years worth to spell:
These hands mean more than my own.

I had to live half a life until I learnt to read it
on her paper palms. The kettle winded,

dry bowls on the shelf, the jab of a cold pin
grazing flecks in a hand that held his still.

Clay Baby

There's no point in telling us about sex, girls like us
were fathered by longing, a stick scraped along

a chest, lonely for something that can't be explained.
Under a jackal-berry tree our mothers sat at five or six,

a mouse-bird chiselling the silence. It was like chipping
a song out of air, just being there, my mother says.

Listening to a croak of heron as if she invented it,
she wondered what it may feel like to call a child's name.

She squished her hands into the squelch and made a clay baby,
shaped me the way a bear licks a clump of fur into a cub.

This is the day girls like us are born, truly, conceived
in a song that has no words yet hummed by any river,

a child watching clay dry, fingers poking our eyes
in our faces, the gouge of our mouths cracked in the sun.

Rose Petal Jelly

The apples drip slow as September
dabbing sun to the rain, juice
slips over the glazed lip of a jug.

Outside, a resilience of roses hold
in the wind. We feel petals open, jagged
caruncles in the corner of our eyes.

One nod and I shin a fence, grab
a second flush in blushing fists.
Mother snips off the bitter white tips

and grins. Some women don't deserve
roses, or know how to use them, she says.

The kitchen smells like a honeymoon.
Only love letters open as slowly
as she lifts the lid, nosing in at the roses

someone's wife didn't pick, all ours,
donating their rubies to our pan.
She holds a sunset and lets it fall

through her sieve. Briefly, the windows
fill with a rosetint. Our used jars
become churches we smash with a spoon.

Caruncle: the red prominence in the inner corner of the eye.

The Cowshed Miracles

This one comes in the autumn,
shoes the shade of fuming brick.
I show her to the cowshed.

She clicks open a case, a peach
inside blushing at her clothes, dip-dyed
in smoke, but for one petticoat.

I see a sole swatch of red, a lone
butterfly asleep in the folds of her
underwear. Sometimes, I'll find

the girl gazing at a wasps' nest lodged
in the joists. Its burnt refuge; the year
a shepherd lost an eye mummified.

In the dun, we oversee lathwork
pinstriping our coats in sunshine,
mushrooms raising pearl umbrellas

under our muddy skirts. Not once do we
speak of war, only potatoes and men –
the correct way to love one who returns.

On a pillow, my fist, I practise a kiss.
She holds a rose to my lips, insists I try again.
If one petal falls, we are doing it wrong.

Against Youth

I am against youth, not yours, not you,
but my own, a bleached scrap hung
on a nail on my door, lilaced by dusk.

Too often it pretends to be a woman
in the dark, snooping for her tall shoes
to attend a dance. I am sick of forgetting

that, in fact, we did not dance, she and I,
or sip cherry cola with a shared straw.
There was no poetry at all, but a snare

in our chests, a pop of music we made
loud enough not to hear our own voices
flinging us off another cliff. I am done

being persuaded to cling to youth.
To hold her hand is to skin myself to fit
into a dress that didn't suit me to start with.

I see that lady out, draw a blind on her eyes
set on some dusty horizon. Let her run, let me
stay in, paper my walls with any creature

I like. I choose sparrows. I choose
to paint my sunrise all over the bricks
with colours I mixed in my own can.

Queen Victoria's Wedding Dress

Tonight is a hundred pins dropped
on black lino, a skitter of stars.
The fog dots a scarf to my hair.

I race on brewery-sluiced paths,
a bolt of moon underfoot, fleet
as cloth running off the roll.

The seamstress is at work still,
a lamp blares in the doorway. I knock,
and a silver fingertip clicks the knob.

Of all the girls she chose me to freeze
into a gown. Be the size of a queen.
I slip on the dress like sea foam.

The seamstress is an orbit of steel,
constellations fly from her fingers,
jab Orion to my bust. I daren't touch,

aware of my sudden white fabric,
hands, the lemon blossom embroidered
over the swell of my heart. She kneels,

lifts my skirt and crawls in, scattered pins
spot the rug. I sway, callus palmed,
thighs satin. Something fits.

Making Love Outside of Chernobyl

Not far from the fence, men with rifles shining
up plums on their uniforms, I undressed in front of you

for the first time since. I heard something wing over us,
wolves born in rooms with polished shoes by the bed.

You folded your shirt on a chair. We did our all not to
think about skin, slowly peeling off our clothes.

The deer are fat, that's something, you said,
stroking my belly. Whiskers fiery as a streak of fawn

in overgrown orchards, crunching bruises, apples rolling
over wildflowers. You circled my breast with a finger.

I saw a falcon stringing a nest to the fire watchtower
outside the school. And the bison are well, I said, hand

on chest curling tracks of my touch into you like a hoof
on a road where animals run on crazed concrete, faster

than they know they can. This is all I saw as you came
inside me, our lips snowflakes, locked, muzzling our cries.

Beatrix Potter's Bed

I never told you how after I saw the sows
birthing I could no longer draw pigs in velvet.
The sound curls around me like a tail, draws me
over to watch you digging. One hand on a spade,
we stare at one another, rabbits shy of strange gardens,
eyes burrowing for cover. The sky is a blue jacket
snared on a fence. Soon, I suppose, we'll try again.
But, now, we have daylight to farm, a glance to bump
into, gazes at one another to snatch. You: wind-raw,
knee-deep in sheep. Me: knuckles radish red/white
kneading dough. Later, we'll peel back the sheets
like squirrels making a raft of sticks, open a basket
and pour all those pictures the day paints of us
over the bed, so full, I can't see room for more.

Joan of Arc

Clutching the sword, I picture my mother,
all spindle and broom chasing wisps
of wool out the door like a ram come undone.

Each soldier bleeds his own way. No two fall
the same, some grip their wounds close
as posies. Others shyly mist the air.

Every man deserves a good death, and I give it.
I kneel and crushed flowers clean my shoes,
my thighs are hassocks tending a last prayer.

So close, a man may sense a breast
under my steel, I lean in, ear a cup held
to dry lips making the shape of home.

The dying speak a language I don't understand.
It sounds like a strand of cotton on a blade.
There's nothing I can tell you about it,

other than the breeze the words make
on my face. It's soft as a sway of poppies
letting go of their skirts in the wind.

The Woman with No Name

I wake and can't remember my name, Mother
veined to my underwear, stitched to my calves.

The sunlight frays his shirt. I scrub, my fingers
falconry gloves, leathered by so much laundering of love.

The cloak is a stone I tie on to throw myself
into the snow. I march, feet ironing moonlight

to the fields, baby kisses stuck in my teeth –
tender rotten meat. Who washes a soldier's clothes,

salts the bloodstains, scours the shame out of cheeks?
There is so much to mend. The firelight tatters night.

Outside, I rub stars on the window, boy-breath iced
to the pane, nose pressed to heroic men, once again.

I warned him not to go in. I can't take my own advice.
The hall smells of sweetbread, a rise and fall of chests.

I lift a sword, an arm, discarded toys on the rug. I hold
a cool hand, each callus on his palm mirrors my own –

our lives knotted to our skin by the kindling axe. Drifting
bed to bed, my steel finger strokes sleeping heads,

blonde cocoons. Red Admirals fly and splash silk
on my dress. And I forget to etch a mother's name

to the shield of each man, my own slips through my fist,
forgiving the latch. I walk out alone. My fingers dry

and uncurl, flakes fall. I leave freckles on the snow.

In Beowulf, *Grendel's mother is never given a name.*

The Loss Adjustors

It happens while we sleep, a man climbs out of bed,
creaks on a tie and tucks a flask of milk into a satchel

like a doctor arriving too late. Gripped in hill shade,
the house waits for someone to adjust our losses

simply as a corset. Once more we'll be able to exhale.
He'll dress, I imagine, in a suit. Footfall soft as wing-skin,

his creep up the path, smile like a doorstep, bevelled
into him by our comings and goings. Of course,

he'll have forms, cursive stingy as spooled twine.
He'll verify the date, clock his pocket-watch, then tell me

the odd fact, like: *briar birds weave cornflowers in thorns.*
To mate they accept they may not survive. And I'll nod,

as if I understand. I'll hold out a hand to be presented
with the mouth of a woman who has all her losses adjusted

and correct. *It was for the best. It wasn't in my destiny*, I'll say,
all the words ladies are supposed to say before they die.

Confession of a Selkie

You can spot a woman who once had a different skin.
Our eyes are mourning lockets set into rockface.
We turn from the lighthouse, the seals carving
a wave into leather, and flap a tarp on the logs.
We keep busy to stop our hands falling off.
The lives we could have lived are charcoal,
rub away as painfully as the freckles on our arms.
You can catch our hearts only in our laughs
that crack into a cackle simply oiling a raincoat.
We make ordinary things our clothes, dip our heads
under pecked kisses to cover the size of our thoughts.
You'd never know unless you saw us peel an egg, roll
the soft boil, that we love you only as a sea-cow sleeps:
one fin paddling always, partly drifting, half awake.

To Catch a Fisherman

The Singer grunts another steel shanty.
Mother puts a foot down on fish skins
bucking the light, an ocean in the room.

It's a fine day to catch a fisherman, let
fog spritz a veil over a squirm of tail, shells
cutting patterns in my chest like dough.

I can cut a fisherman out of his boat,
if I sit still long enough, dangle the bait of
a song off a rock to a man looking for a story

to reel. There's none who won't come,
reach out for a myth to writhe in his hands.
I serenade the speck of my house, sad

as a woman who can't dance, wind rinsing
out recollections of sinking in the bath
pretending to be half-anemone, half-girl.

The keel of my voice creaks a song
of Mother's bad back, logs aching to be lugged,
a cold foot in bed inching for a warm sole.

She catches the lone fisherman in her net,
a sprat of man who sees me strip off my tail,
harpoon licking the hollow in his neck.

Together we bundle him back to the house,
Mother's laugh is a shoal. It slips over us,
a glint of mermaids bringing the silver home.

Note in a Bottle

Let us say no more than fits in a bottle, go
no further than the moon takes us. I look out to sea
and fathom my chances of bumping into your boat

to launch a thought. Caught in your net, kelped,
you may find me, this bottle you swigged, snogged
dandelion 'n' burdock off the neck. I thread

myself inside one heartbeat at a time, nerves nylon,
the matchstick ship of a more patient man. I won't
fling my worries at you, but cast out one line alone.

I miss you. And love is a storm warning for some,
the stories of fisherman's wives are wrecks in my veins.
I say nothing, but stash glassware, screw on a lid

and wait for a reply. If you find me, whisper into a shell
I can pick up on the beach. I'll lay it on my pillow
tonight, and fancy I hear you breathing, so I may sleep.

Fiddling the Gas

My father never gave me the stars, but he came
to my first flat to knock the moon on its back.
I let him in, snow on his hair fusing to grey as he bent
on one knee and I offered him coffee – a stranger,
a daughter, unsure what to say. It seems we waited
for the plumber all our lives, my mother and I inched
through sleeping bag Decembers, peered into hatches
at dead boilers, the light blown out of their eyes.
He drilled the cast and smeared black wax on the hole
to disguise our partnership in crime. It was like skating
on Saturn, the way we gazed at the dial. Just once,
the world span on a flipped coin in our pockets, simple
as stopped clocks in our hands. Together, we knelt to see
steel turn out winter, the meter rolling back time.

The Poet's Last Will and Testament

I bequeath to you daybreak upholstering my chair,
a map of light on the rug. And birds, I shan't name,
but allow to make their own introductions, peck
a pause to the window I saw through. You may find
the view worn as a painter's brush. Touch it, never stop
looking. Listen for soft collisions, notice bees and recall
your childish felt pens, swapping the yellow and black lids.
I leave you the art of snails on walls, slow as palm readers
stroking life and love to a hand. Don't be surprised to find
faces and hearts in my room, knotted to the oak desk.
Its weeping is done, sap dry, I promise it will be, in time.
This old chair will learn the shape of another's idle hour.
Fill it, roll a page of moonlight into an Olivetti, let your name
on the cork overlap mine. I can give you only this. Now.

Postscript to a Note in a Bottle

I picture you, Bottle, still at sea, paper words
swallowed, spat, lapping at a tongue of moonlight.

His sleeping hand finds me and I think of you;
rim of scratches, sharp edges rubbed into sea glass.

The Book of Tides Closes

The slack-tide is the worst, curled on my side
I press a conch to one ear, as if, I may hear
a cough of men washing up on the shore.

The curtains never did meet. Daybreak hauls
me to flaming windows, sandpiper slow, footsteps
gathering sand, boots concreted to my dance.

The ships don't come in like they did.
No waltz of fishermen hang on my every word,
my face an opal in a lobster-claw clasp,

suspended to smack on a kiss as if I was
the cod of the catch. The magic is gone,
my bones no longer inkle for storms.

And still I stare out at lead wings, a scrat
of gulls on the outhouse, beaks blotted
in crescents red as kisses that won't wash.

I listen to bird squall like drowned men
rearranging old squabbles all day, as if one may
finally find the right words, get the last one in.

Acknowledgements

I would like to thank the competitions where some of the poems appeared: The *Mslexia* Poetry Competition (The Book of Tides, winner), The Charles Causley Prize (The Museum of Water, winner 2014), The Essex Poetry Prize (winner), The Cardiff International Poetry Competition (commended 2014), The Phillip Larkin Prize (commended 2015). The Hippocrates Prize (commended 2014.).

I'd also like to express my appreciation to the editors of the journals, magazines, blogs, and anthologies who were kind enough to publish some of the poems: *And Other Poems, Agenda, Bare Fiction, Clear Poetry, Elbow Room, Envoi, Furies* anthology (For Booksake), *Hallelujah For 50ft Women* (Bloodaxe, 2015), *Ink, Sweat, and Tears, Interpreter's House, The Rialto, The Everyday Poet: Poems to Live By* (October 2016) *Magma, Ofi Press Journal, Poems in Which, Peony Moon, Popshot, Prole, Slim Volume, Stare's Nest, Three Drops from the Cauldron – Full Moon & Foxglove: an anthology of witches and witchcraft* (2016), *Under the Radar, The Morning Star – Well Versed, Your One Phone Call.*

I am grateful to Jo Bell, the 52 project, and the suggestion I could think about a collection, without which this book wouldn't exist. Thank you to everyone in the 52 group who offered me encouragement and kindness. These small acts of support made me come back to poetry when I had decided to quit. Many thanks to Jane Commane for her all her work, tireless enthusiasm, and for giving me a chance. Thank you.